Contents

AMUSEMENT PARK MATH

A Ten-Minute Daily Math Adventure

Written and Illustrated by Michael Cain

Copyright ©2007 Prufrock Press Inc.

Edited by Lacy Elwood
Illustrated by Michael Cain
Production Design by Marjorie Parker

ISBN-13: 978-1-59363-291-5
ISBN-10: 1-59363-291-6

At the time of this book's publication, all facts and figures cited are the most current available; all telephone numbers, addresses, and Web site URLs are accurate and active; all publications, organizations, Web sites, and other resources exist as described in this book; and all have been verified. The authors and Prufrock Press make no warranty or guarantee concerning the information and materials given out by organizations or content found at Web sites, and we are not responsible for any changes that occur after this book's publication. If you find an error or believe that a resource listed here is not as described, please contact Prufrock Press.

Prufrock Press Inc.
P.O. Box 8813
Waco, TX 76714-8813
Phone: (800) 998-2208
Fax: (800) 240-0333
http://www.prufrock.com

Teacher's Guide

The increased emphasis on standards-based test scores may support the need for consistent practice of math fundamentals, but it is undisputable that strong basic skills and problem-solving experience play a role in future math understanding and success. I am a firm believer in the idea that practice leads to mastery. I do not think there are many teachers that will argue this point. What can be a point of concern is where a teacher can find the time to practice fundamentals and problem solving and still cover the vast amount of content to be tested.

I created *Amusement Park Math* to meet the needs of teachers like myself who have too many demands and not enough time. This book is an easy way to provide students with basic skill and problem-solving practice. Each page of the book provides four fundamental skill practice problems that directly relate to the page's problem-solving situation. To add more interest and engagement for the student, the story problems in this book fit together to form an ongoing narrative.

The much-maligned story problem has often been the bane of many a math student. For the teacher, trying to get students to attempt the problem is tantamount to pulling teeth. The story problems in this book are specifically designed to engage the student. Ongoing characters and a realistic, yet fanciful, storyline connect the student with the problems. Students will become familiar with the characters and develop an interest in their lives. This interest will spark a desire in the student to solve the problem and to look forward to the next installment in the story. Students will get basic practice in math fundamentals in the practice problems, but they also will get continuous exposure to problem-solving situations and the chance to develop their reading for information skills.

Amusement Park Math is designed to be seamlessly integrated into any part of a lesson or curriculum. It can be used at the beginning of a class as a lead-in for a day's lesson or as a review of the previous day's lesson. It can be used as a way to bring a class to closure after a lesson on a specific fundamental skill. It can help focus a class after any type of disruption, such as a fire drill or assembly. By using three or four pages at once, it can be an emergency lesson plan used by a substitute. The problems also can be added to homework assignments. This book is a versatile resource that can assist a teacher in a variety of ways.

Amusement Park Math is not meant to replace any part of a lesson. It is designed to add enjoyment to a class. Its ease of use and versatility make its integration into a daily routine easy and effortless. I created this book to help teachers and students develop a passion for story problems, practice basic skills, prepare for standard-based testing, and integrate reading into the math classroom. This book is designed to be used in grades 4–6 and can also be used for intervention in grades 7 and 8.

Each chapter is geared to a basic skill that is a fundamental part of any math curriculum. The topics in the book are universal and coincide with state and national standards including the exploration of number forms, number operations, number sense, data analysis, and problem solving. Using *Amusement Park Math* every day helps develop and maintain a consistent classroom structure and focus students on the lesson of the day. The cartoon illustrations and engaging characters will provide a comfort level for students that will allow a teacher to pursue more challenging topics and a more rigorous program. The ongoing storyline will help increase the level of interest in the student and stimulate problem solving, imagination, and creativity.

I designed this book to meet my needs as a teacher. My students have enjoyed using it and have consistently shown improvement in their basic math skills, problem-solving fundamentals, and reading comprehension. I hope it does the same for you and your students.

Part I: Addition and Subtraction

Workout 1: Addition, Interpreting Charts

Find the sum.

1. $64 + 25 =$ _____

2. $512 + 196 =$ _____

3.
$$\begin{array}{r} 345 \\ +54 \\ \hline \end{array}$$

4.
$$\begin{array}{r} 304 \\ +762 \\ \hline \end{array}$$

Word Problem

5. The carnival has closed and the performers of General Thumb's Theater of Thrills are out of a job. General Thumb adds up the last week's ticket sales to determine how much money his group has earned during the week. Use the chart to determine the total earnings for the week.

Day	Earnings
Saturday	$375
Sunday	$298
Monday	Closed
Tuesday	Closed
Wednesday	$103
Thursday	$175
Friday	$295

Workout 2: Addition, Subtraction, Interpreting Charts

Find the sum.

1. 2,576
     + 153

2. $2,978 + 2,112 =$ _____

Find the difference.

3. 4,569
     −1,521

4. $5,672 - 974 =$ _____

5. What answer is the greatest? _____

Word Problem

6. General Thumb has kept a record of all the money his troupe has earned during the past year. He is afraid that the troupe has made less than they did the year before. Last year, the troupe earned $81,987. General Thumb wants to compare this year's earnings with that amount. Use the chart to calculate the troupe's total earnings for the year and compare that answer with last year's earnings. How much less money did the troupe earn this year?

Months	Earnings
January–March	$14,146
April–June	$16,394
July–September	$25,192
October–December	$18,288

Name_____ Date:_____

Workout 3: Addition, Subtraction, Interpreting Data

List these numbers from least to greatest.

1. 179, 184, 121, 98, 156 _____

2. 724, 754, 703, 698, 749 _____

Compare the numbers using < or >.

3. $526 ◯ $462   **4.** 2,548 ◯ 3,659

Word Problem

5. Each member of General Thumb's Theater of Thrills spends a different amount of money on food each week. Zambul the Strongman spends $117, General Thumb spends $96, Minerva the Mysterious spends $75, Flying Freda spends $86, and Rosco the Clown spends $101. (a) What is the total of all their weekly food expenses? (b) Which person spends the most on food? (c) Which person spends the least on food? (d) How much more money does General Thumb spend on food than Minerva each week?

Name_____ Date:_____

Workout 4: Addition, Subtraction, Money

Find the difference.

1. $700 − $596 = _____

2. $1,500 − $871 = _____

3. $1,200
 − $635
 _____

4. $2,000
 − $1,832
 _____

Word Problem

5. General Thumb's troupe is about to begin their search for a new place to perform, and they decide to contemplate their options over lunch. General Thumb buys some peanut butter for $3, grape jelly for $4, bread for $2, and milk for $3. He pays for the food with a $10 bill and a $5 bill. What is the amount of his change?

Workout 5: Addition, Subtraction, Interpreting Data

Find the difference.

1. $5,789
      – $2,561

2. $13,741
      – $8,294

3. $4,218 – $3,954 = _____

4. $14,765 – $12,519 = _____

Word Problem

5. Meanwhile, in the nearby city of Modest Lake, the city council is holding an emergency meeting. The community's historic amusement park has lost money for the past 5 years. (a) Use the chart below to determine the total losses the park has suffered during the past 5 years. (b) In which year did the park lose the most money?

Year	2001	2002	2003	2004	2005
Money Lost	$11,881	$7,854	$9,746	$11,819	$11,188

Name_____ Date:_____

Workout 6: Addition, Interpreting Data

Find the sum.

1. $526 + 475 + 641 =$ _____

2. $1,529 + 546 + 755 =$ _____

3.
$$\begin{array}{r} 3,564 \\ 857 \\ +\ 233 \\ \hline \end{array}$$

4.
$$\begin{array}{r} 6,532 \\ 1,567 \\ +1,030 \\ \hline \end{array}$$

5. Of the above answers, which is the largest sum?

Word Problem

6. Modest Lake Amusement Park is in debt and may have to close. Because the park has not been able to pay its bills for some time, it has had to borrow money from the town for the past 5 years. (a) Use the chart below to determine the total amount of money the park has borrowed from the town. (b) In which year did the park borrow the least amount of money? (c) In which year did the park borrow the most amount of money?

Year	2001	2002	2003	2004	2005
Amount Borrowed	$32,500	$23,250	$29,900	$23,990	$32,050

Workout 7: Addition, Subtraction, Interpreting Data

Compare the numbers using < or >.

1. 645 ◯ 723

2. 471 ◯ 671

3. 1,562 ◯ 2,197

4. 8,971 ◯ 9,897

Word Problem

5. The Modest Lake Amusement Park has borrowed $141,690 from the town. Mr. Gregory, Modest Lake's school principal, is the chairman of the town council. He has a chart that lists the other debts the park has accumulated. (a) Determine the total of the park's other debts. (b) What's the difference between the total amount of other debts and the amount of money the park owes the town?

Other Park Debt	
Repair bills	$16,890
Insurance	$26,789
Bank Loans	$53,823
Unpaid wages	$11,334
Food bills	$14,705

Workout 8: Addition, Subtraction, Interpreting Data

Find the next two numbers in each pattern.

1. 2, 4, 6, 8, _____, _____

2. 3, 6, 9, 12, _____, _____

3. 265, 260, 255, 250, _____, _____

4. 120, 116, 112, 108, _____, _____

Word Problem

5. The park has not paid its taxes for the past 3 years. The town will charge the park a penalty for each year it did not pay its taxes. The first year's penalty is $1,200, the second year's penalty is $2,400, and the third year's penalty is $4,800. At the emergency town council meeting, Dr. Chin presented data that showed the local amusement park already owes the community $73,945 in back taxes. This year the park owes the town $24,648 in taxes, plus a new penalty for the fourth year. (a) From the pattern, determine this year's tax penalty. (b) Then find the total amount of money the park owes in taxes and tax penalties.

Workout 9: Addition, Subtraction, Interpreting Data

Find the sum.

1. $352 + 167 =$ _____

2. $189 + 315 =$ _____

3.   537
        $+ 231$

4.   986
        $+ 259$

Word Problem

5. The carnival has closed, and the performing troupe must search for a new place to work. They are not sure how much gas they have left in their truck, so they want to travel to the nearest town. Rosco the Clown and General Thumb use a map to try to determine the nearest town. Estimate the distance from their starting point to the nearest town using the map below.

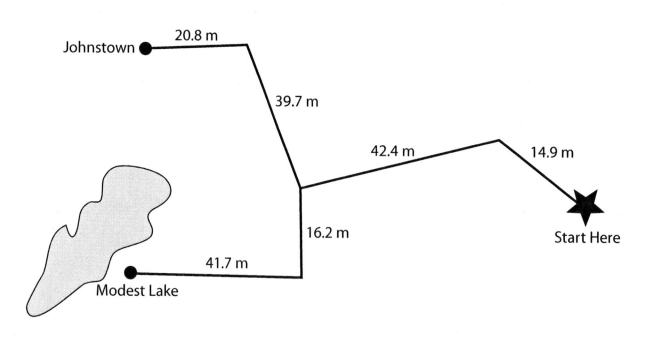

Workout 10: Addition, Subtraction, Interpreting Data

Find the sum.

1. $15 + 15 + 15 + 15 + 15 + 15 + 15 + 15 + 15 =$ _____

2. $76 + 76 + 76 + 76 =$ _____

Find the difference.

3. $\begin{array}{r} 64 \\ -22 \\ \hline \end{array}$

4. $\begin{array}{r} 98 \\ -12 \\ \hline \end{array}$

Word Problem

5. General Thumb and his friends are driving toward Modest Lake, which is about 115 miles from their current location. The truck they are using gets about 21 miles to the gallon. If they have 5 gallons of gas in the truck, about how far away from Modest Lake will they be when the truck runs out of gas?

Workout 11: Addition, Subtraction, Multiplication

Find the difference.

1. $200
    − $52
    ―――

2. $500
    − $298
    ―――

3. $6.00 − $5.32 = _____

4. $10.00 − $7.16 = _____

Word Problem

5. After an emergency town council meeting, Farmer Harrison, the town's treasurer, stops at the Gas 'n' Go to tell some friends about the financial problems of the local amusement park. The story is quite long, so he buys everyone a soda to quench their thirst. The soda machine has 6 rows of soda and each row holds 8 bottles.
Farmer Harrison buys 6 bottles. If the rows were full, how many bottles of soda are left in the machine?

Workout 12: Addition, Subtraction, Multiplication

Find the sum.

1. $2 + $5 + $7 + $3 = _____   **2.** $29 + $27 + $26 + $22 = _____

Find the difference.

3. $800   **4.** $1,200
     − $622   − $633

Word Problem

5. As luck would have it, General Thumb's truck runs out of gas. He and is friends are stranded 10 miles from the nearest town. The group gathers up their money and sends Zambul the Strongman to get the gas. The group gives Zambul three $1 bills and two $5 bills. Gas costs $3 a gallon at the Gas 'n' Go. Zambul buys 4 gallons. How much money does he have left?

Name_____ Date:_____

Workout 13: Addition, Rounding

Find the sum.

1. 51,263
   6,758
+ 2,164
_____

2. $34,239 + 12,591 + 1,884 =$ _____

Round to the nearest thousand's place.

3. 31,564 _____

4. 648,239 _____

Word Problem

5. At the Gas 'n' Go, a group of townsfolk are discussing the financial troubles of their local amusement park. Farmer Harrison lists all the renovations the park needs. (a) Find the total cost of the renovations. (b) Round your answer to the nearest thousand.

Ride	Ferris Wheel	The Coaster	The Fun House	The Log Run
Cost to Upgrade	$52,972	$27,230	$19,645	$13,649

Workout 14: Interpreting Data, Rounding

Round each number to the nearest hundred's place.

1. 9,428 _____

2. 3,196 _____

3. 16,035 _____

4. 19,715 _____

5. Order the rounded numbers from Numbers 1–4 from least to greatest.

Word Problem

6. Farmer Harrison looks at the figures for the renovations to the town's amusement park. In order to get a clearer picture of the park's problems, he needs to create a chart and list the renovation costs from least to greatest. Using the table below, (a) round the cost for each renovation to the nearest hundred and (b) list them from least to greatest.

Ride	Ferris Wheel	The Coaster	The Fun House	The Log Run
Cost to Upgrade	$52,972	$27,230	$19,645	$13,649

Name_____ Date:_____

Workout 15: Addition, Subtraction, Interpreting Data

Solve each problem, finding either the sum or the difference.

1. 32
    + 26
    ___

2. 64
    − 52
    ___

3. 88 − 65 = _____

4. 64 + 33 = _____

Word Problem

5. The financial troubles of the local amusement park couldn't have come at a worse time for the town's treasurer. It is harvest season, and Farmer Harrison is short on help. He has 32 acres of crops. He grows strawberries, apples, and peaches. He has 16 acres of apples and 2 more acres of strawberries than peaches. How many acres of each crop does he have?

Name_____ Date:_____

Workout 16: Addition, Subtraction, Interpreting Data

Solve each problem.

1. $56 + 22 - 16 = $ _____

2. $32 + 45 - 20 = $ _____

3. $84 - 32 + 64 = $ _____

4. $52 - 12 + 50 = $ _____

Word Problem

5. Zambul the Strongman is on his way back with gasoline to help his stranded friends. A kindly farmer gives him a ride. During the ride back to the truck, Zambul talks about his carnival experiences. He has spent 22 years performing in circuses, sideshows, and wrestling matches. He has worked 2 more years in circuses than in sideshows, and he has worked 6 more years in the circuses than in wrestling matches. How many years has he worked in each profession?

Workout 17: Addition, Subtraction, Money

Find the sum.

1. $1,648
+ $1,324

2. $3,624 + $1,268 = _____

Find the difference.

3. $52,634
− $3,964

4. $61,301 − $9,630 = _____

Word Problem

5. Zambul the Strongman and his friends need a place to stay. Farmer Harrison needs some help on his farm. If Zambul can get his friends to help Farmer Harrison, they can stay at the farm for free and earn some money. This year, Farmer Harrison will pay his workers $1,075 more than last year's total. Last year, Farmer Harrison paid his workers a total of $3,254 to help get his crops to the market. If he hopes to sell his crops for $78,925 this year, how much money will he earn from his crops after he pays his workers?

Workout 18: Addition, Subtraction, Interpreting Data

Find the difference.

1. $6,258
 −$235
_____

2. $4,264
 −$638
_____

3. $2,198 − $920 = _____

4. $5,695 − $998 = _____

Word Problem

5. General Thumb gladly accepts Farmer Harrison's offer of a place to stay and a chance to earn some money. General Thumb negotiates a deal with Farmer Harrison that includes free meals in exchange for extra work. It will take 2 weeks to get the crops to market. If the troupe had to buy its own food, it would cost them $475 a week to eat. Farmer Harrison is paying them $3,254, plus an extra $1,075 to work for him. If General Thumb had *not* made a deal that included meals, how much money would be left from the troupe's earnings after they paid for food costs?

Workout 19: Addition, Subtraction

Find the sum.

1.   566
      +625
      ‾‾‾‾

2.   124
      +158
      ‾‾‾‾

3. Subtract the largest of the two sums above from 2,536.

4. $341 + 212 =$ _____

5. $274 + 641 =$ _____

Word Problem

6. General Thumb and his troupe set up camp near Farmer Harrison's barn. Harrison gives them a 1,000 square foot field in which to pitch their tents. Zambul's tent takes up 400 square feet. General Thumb's tent takes up 144 square feet. Minerva and Freda share a 225 square foot tent, and Rosco the Clown has a 169 square foot tent. (a) Is there enough room to pitch all their tents? (b) If yes, how much extra room do they have leftover? If no, how much more room do they need?

Workout 20: Addition, Subtraction, Multiplication

Find the sum.

1. 52
    +49
   ‾‾‾

2. 74
    +61
   ‾‾‾

Solve the problems, using addition and subtraction.

3. $23 + 45 - 12 =$ _____

4. $54 + 54 + 54 - 108 =$ _____

Word Problem

5. Farmer Harrison's mother lives in a small cottage on the farm. She is excited to have guests, so she prepares a big meal to welcome General Thumb and his troupe. She bakes four of her special blueberry pies. Each pie requires 28 ounces of blueberries. She has 64 ounces of fresh berries, and 64 ounces of frozen berries. If she uses all of the fresh berries up first, how many ounces of frozen berries will she have leftover after the pies are made?

Part II: Multiplication

Workout 21: Multiplication, Two-Digit Numbers

Find the product.

1. $12 \times 6 =$ _____

2. $51 \times 4 =$ _____

3. $14 \times 7 =$ _____

4. $46 \times 5 =$ _____

Word Problem

5. The apples in the orchard are ripe and ready for harvest. Flying Freda has taken on the job of picking the apples. Because Freda can reach the very top of the trees, more apples are picked this season than ever before. Freda picked 37 apples from the top of 5 trees. How many apples did she pick?

Workout 22: Multiplication, Two-Digit Numbers

Find the product.

1. 64
   ×9
   ___

2. 96
   ×7
   ___

3. 25 × 6 = _____

4. 82 × 8 = _____

Word Problem

5. The best apples are located at the top of the trees, where only Flying Freda can pick them. She picks so many champion grade apples that Farmer Harrison plans to pack them up into special boxes and offer them for sale on his Web site. There are 24 champion grade apples per box. The first day the Web site gets 3 orders. One order is for 2 boxes, another order is for 3 boxes, and the last order is for 4 boxes. How many apples are needed to fill the orders?

Workout 23: Multiplication, Three-Digit Numbers

Find the product.

1. 211
   $\times\ 5$

2. 306
   $\times\ 7$

3. $526 \times 3 =$ _____

4. $612 \times 9 =$ _____

Word Problem

5. The peach orchard has 344 trees. General Thumb checks the trees to determine which ones have peaches ripe enough to pick. He will wrap 6 feet of yellow ribbon around each tree that has ripe peaches. How many feet of ribbon will he need to have enough to wrap around every tree?

Workout 24: Multiplication, Addition

Find the product.

1. 267
   $\times$ 2
   ___

2. $267 \times 4 =$ _____

3. $267 \times 6 =$ _____

4. 267
   $\times$ 8
   ___

Word Problem

5. Rosco the Clown sorts the peaches into two categories: those for making jelly and those for canning. He puts the jelly-making peaches into 623 rows of 6 peaches each. He puts the canning peaches into 842 rows of 8 peaches each. How many peaches are there altogether?

Workout 25: Multiplication, Addition, Subtraction

Solve the problems using multiplication, addition, or subtraction.

1. 63
     × 4
  ——

2.   420
     −152
    ——

3. 54 + 16 + 39 = _____

4. 82 × 5 = _____

Word Problem

5. The strawberry harvest is outstanding this year. Four acres produced 101 pints each. Four acres produced 87 pints each, and four acres produced 99 pints each. (a) What is the total amount of pints of strawberries produced? (b) What is the difference in pints of strawberries between the four acres that produced the most and the four acres that produced the least?

Workout 26: Multiplication, Three-Digit Numbers With Zero

Find the product.

1. $104 \times 8 =$ _____

2. $905 \times 5 =$ _____

3. $103 \times 3 =$ _____

4. $506 \times 6 =$ _____

Word Problem

5. Farmer Harrison's special-blend strawberry fields are filled with big red berries. He picks a total of 108 pints of strawberries from each of his 7 acres. If he sells each pint for $3, how much money will he make?

Workout 27: Multiplication, Subtraction

Find the product.

1. $\begin{array}{r} 300 \\ \times\,15 \\ \hline \end{array}$

2. $\begin{array}{r} 200 \\ \times\,18 \\ \hline \end{array}$

3. $12 \times 10 \times 5 =$ _____

4. $30 \times 15 \times 10 =$ _____

5. What is the difference between the answer to Number 1 and the answer to Number 3?

Word Problem

6. Moving hay bales is heavy work. The bales of hay in the field must be stored in the barn. Zambul uses the job as his daily workout. He carries 19 hay bales that weigh 120 pounds each. He carries a 16 hay bales that weigh 90 pounds each, and he carries 12 hay bales that weigh 106 pounds each. What is the difference in weight between the total weight of all the hay bales and the 19 bales that weigh 120 pounds?

Workout 28: Multiplication, Four-Digit Numbers

Find the product.

1. 1,524
  × 8

2. 3,941
  × 7

3. $1,357 \times 2 =$ _____

4. $5,649 \times 3 =$ _____

Word Problem

5. Farmer Harrison harvests a section of his cornfield. He will store his corn in six different silos. He fills 3 of his silos with 8,009 pounds of corn each. He fills 2 of his silos with 5,134 pounds of corn each and the last remaining silo he fills with 9,786 pounds of corn. What is the total weight of corn in all six silos?

Workout 29: Multiplication, Subtraction

Find the product.

1. $294
   × 6

2. $294
   × 60

3. $492 × 20 = _____

4. Find the difference between the answer to Number 2 and the answer to Number 3.

Word Problem

5. General Thumb helps Farmer Harrison with the daily milk collection and the sale of the milk to a local dairy. Farmer Harrison sold his milk for $488 a day. General Thumb renegotiates the deal with the dairy for Farmer Harrison, and now Farmer Harrison gets $1,509 for 3 days worth of milk. How much more money will Farmer Harrison make in 30 days with the new price?

Workout 30: Multiplication, Subtraction

Find the product.

1. 22
  $\times\,15$
  _____

2. $87 \times 15 =$ _____

Find the difference.

3. 9,254
  $-\,4,142$
  _____

4. $7,208 - 6,211 =$ _____

Word Problem

5. Minerva the Mysterious is not very good at farm work. However, she is very good at cooking. Together, she and Ma Harrison prepare lunch and dinner for all others on the farm. Ma Harrison has 16 recipe books. Each book has 156 recipes. If Minerva reads 84 recipes every day for 7 days, how many recipes will she have left to read if she wants to read all of the recipes in Ma Harrison's books?

Name_____ Date:_____

Workout 31: Multiplication, Addition, Interpreting Data

Find the product.

1. $323 \times 13 =$ _____

2. $632 \times 11 =$ _____

Find the sum.

3.   25,663
       $+ 21,169$

4.   31,778
       $+ 67,018$

Word Problem

5. There are 3 pigs barns on the farm. Barn A has 24 pens with 4 pigs in each. Barn B has 12 pens that each hold 6 pigs. Barn. C has 9 pens with 12 pigs in each of the pens. (a) How many pigs are in each barn? (b) How many pigs are in all the barns combined. (c) List barns in order from least to greatest number of pigs.

Workout 32: Multiplication, Subtraction

Find the difference.

1. 16,345
     $-\,7,612$

2. $13,691 - 11,285 =$ _____

Find the product.

3. $5 \times 12 \times 6 =$ _____

4. $3 \times 3 \times 3 \times 3 =$ _____

Word Problem

5. The chickens on the farm produced 979 dozen eggs last year. This year, Farmer Harrison has decreased the number of chickens on his farm and expects to only get 779 dozen eggs. (a) What is the total number of eggs produced last year? (b) What is the total number of eggs Farmer Harrison expects this year? (c) What is the difference in the amounts?

Workout 33: Multiplication

Find the product.

1. $193 \times 16 =$ _____

2. $142 \times 13 =$ _____

3. 291
$\times\, 25$

4. 324
$\times\, 28$

Word Problem

5. Most of the rides and attractions of Modest Lake Amusement Park are in need of repair and upgrades. The Paratrooper is one of the oldest and most reliable rides. In the 23 years it has been in operation, it has never been down for repairs. Each year it runs 125 days without a breakdown. What is the total number of days it has been operational in its 23 years of existence?

Workout 34: Multiplication, Addition

Find the product.

1. 10
    $\times 6$

2.   4
    $\times 6$

3. $7 \times 8 =$ _____

4. $3 \times 5 =$ _____

5. Find the sum of all four products above.

Word Problem

6. The Paratrooper has 16 rider pods. Each pod can hold up to 4 riders. On one ride operation, there are 8 pods with 3 riders, 5 pods with 4 riders, and 2 pods with 2 riders. How many people went for a ride?

Workout 35: Multiplication

Find the product.

1. $\begin{array}{r} 12 \\ \times 15 \\ \hline \end{array}$

2. $\begin{array}{r} 21 \\ \times 11 \\ \hline \end{array}$

3. $22 \times 19 =$ _____

4. $20 \times 13 =$ _____

Word Problem

5. The Merry-Go-Round is one of the park's star attractions and is more than 100 years old. It has 12 ride sessions an hour. If about 26 people ride it each session, about how many people ride it in an hour?

Workout 36: Multiplication, Addition, Subtraction

Find the product.

1. 15
       × 8
       ___

2. 17 × 6 = _____

Solve the problems using addition or subtraction.

3. 5,004 − 2,583 = _____

4.   31,891
       +19,784
       _____

Word Problem

5. All the carousel mounts are hand painted, and they are each unique. There are 12 rows of 3 mounts and 12 rows of 2 mounts. Thirty-eight of the mounts are horses. The rest of the mounts are different types of animals. How many mounts are not horses?

Workout 37: Multiplication, Subtraction

Find the difference.

1. 12,400
−6,299
‾‾‾‾‾‾

2. $18,007 - 11,365 =$ _____

Find the product.

3. $48 \times 24 =$ _____

4. $34 \times 27 =$ _____

Word Problem

5. The Roto Rocket is a common ride at the amusement park, but it is closed for overhaul 3 days a week. The park is only open everyday for 24 weeks. How many days is the ride in operation?

Workout 38: Multiplication, Time, Interpreting Data

How many hours have passed in each problem below?

1. 8 p.m. to 2 a.m. _____

2. 9 a.m. to 4 p.m. _____

Find the product.

3. $800 \times 200 =$ _____

4. $500 \times 300 =$ _____

Word Problem

5. Morris and Ethel Needamire hold the park record for taking the most rides in one day. Including loading and unloading passengers, their favorite ride takes 6 minutes. The Needamires rode their favorite ride every time it ran on the day they set the record. If the park opens at 10 a.m. and closes at 10 p.m., how many rides did each of the Needamires take to set the record?

Workout 39: Multiplication, Addition

Find the product.

1. 290
$\times\, 60$

2. 650
$\times\, 40$

3. $710 \times 30 =$ _____

4. $450 \times 80 =$ _____

5. Find the sum of all four products above.

Word Problem

5. Since 1949, the Tilt-A-Whirl has given the park's patrons an enjoyable experience. The chains that drive the ride have four links per foot. There is a 70-foot chain and a 50-foot chain driving the ride. How many total links are in both chains?

Workout 40: Multiplication

Find the product.

1.   21
     $\times 12$
     ___

2.   71
     $\times 17$
     ___

3. $35 \times 36 =$ _____

4. $62 \times 63 =$ _____

Word Problem

5. The Tilt-A-Whirl carriages are in need of paint jobs. The ride has 12 carriages. Each carriage will take 4 hours to paint. The painter will be paid $7 an hour. Determine how much money is needed to pay the painter for the job.

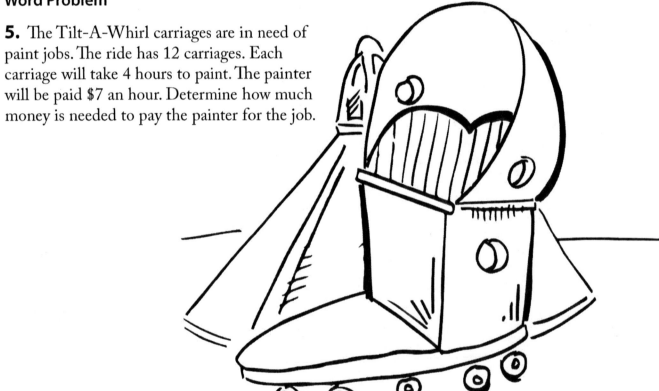

Workout 41: Multiplication, Subtraction

Find the product.

1. 11
    × 7
   ‾‾‾‾

2. 15
    × 4
   ‾‾‾‾

3. $38 \times 5 =$ _____

4. $28 \times 9 =$ _____

5. Add the products above and subtract their total from 600.

Word Problem

6. The Aero-Drones have two 15-foot chains connecting them to the main body of the ride. The park has 300 yards of chain. The ride has eight Aero-Drones. (a) Does the park have enough chain to replace all the chains holding the Aero-Drones? (b) Determine how much extra chain they have or how much more chain they need.

Workout 42: Multiplication, Subtraction, Money

Find the product.

1. $\$75 \times 40 =$ _____

2. $\$113 \times 60 =$ _____

3. $\begin{array}{r} \$95 \\ \times\, \$25 \\ \hline \end{array}$

4. $\begin{array}{r} \$146 \\ \times\, \$88 \\ \hline \end{array}$

5. Add the products above and subtract them from $25,700.

Word Problem

6. The eight Aero-Drones each have two large wings. Each wing is made out of two sheets of aluminum. Each sheet has a cost of $120. The park has $6,000 to spend to replace the wings. How many wings can the park replace?

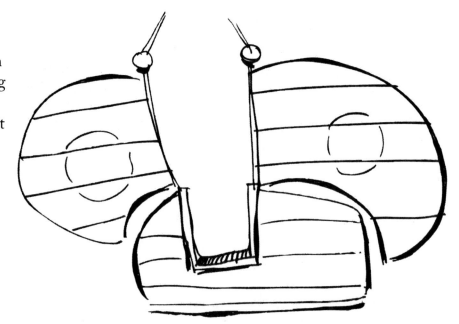

Workout 43: Multiplication, Division

Find the product.

1.   29
      $\times 12$
      _____

2.   38
      $\times 35$
      _____

3. $52 \times 6 =$ _____

4. $47 \times 4 =$ _____

Word Problem

5. The Ferris Wheel has had a lot of problems this season. Recently, it broke down and its passengers were stuck at the top. A hand crank had to be used to move the Ferris Wheel so the passengers could get out. It takes three turns of the crank to lower the wheel one foot. How many times must the crank be turned to lower the wheel 65 feet?

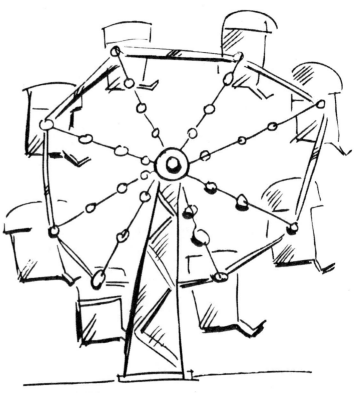

Workout 44: Multiplication, Subtraction

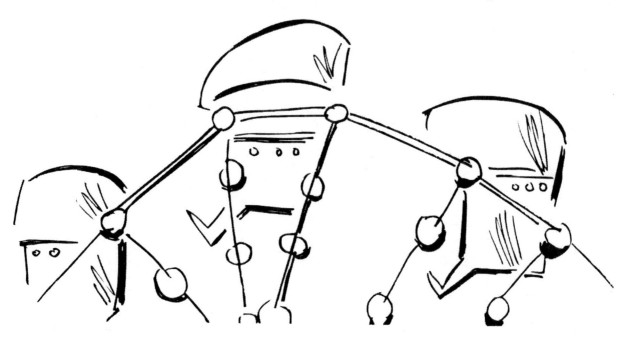

Find the difference.

1.   3,652
         − 1,571
         ———

2. 4,297 − 2,533 = _____

Find the product.

3. $368 \times 4 =$ _____

4.   421
       × 3
       ———

Word Problem

5. The Ferris Wheel has eight carriages. Each carriage weighs 234 pounds. The Ferris Wheel has a maximum weight capacity of 4,000 pounds. Determine the maximum weight for passengers that the Ferris Wheel can accommodate.

Workout 45: Multiplication, Subtraction, Money

Find the difference.

1. $61,534
      − $41,791

2. $52,971 − $13,568 = _____

Find the product.

3. $16,971
    ×   4

4. $21,358 × 3 = _____

Word Problem

5. The Starblazer ride was purchased 5 years ago. Modest Lake made five payments of $31,000 each on the ride. The ride has earned an average of $28,500 for its five seasons at the park. Determine the total difference between the cost and the 5-year earnings.

Name_____ Date:_____

Workout 46: Multiplication

Find the product.

1. $62 \times 23 =$ _____

2. $37 \times 19 =$ _____

3.   58
       $\times 36$
       —

4.   87
       $\times 52$
       —

Word Problem

5. The original park management purchased the Moon Rocket ride 20 years ago. To this day, it remains unfinished. A problem with the hydraulic system prevents it from being operational. The ride has 98 different hydraulic cables. The hydraulic cables have an average length of 67 feet. Determine the total length of the hydraulic cables.

Workout 47: Multiplication, Subtraction

Find the product.

1. $6 \times 7 =$ _____

2. $\begin{array}{r} 8 \\ \times\, 4 \\ \hline \end{array}$

Find the difference.

3. $\begin{array}{r} 56 \\ -\, 32 \\ \hline \end{array}$

4. $74 - 51 =$ _____

Word Problem

5. The bumper cars are always a popular attraction at the amusement park. The attraction started with 46 cars About three cars have broken each year for the past 4 years. As the cars broke, they were removed and never replaced. How many cars remain?

Workout 48: Multiplication, Subtraction

Find the product.

1. $2,597
   $\times \quad 21$

2. $3,628
   $\times \quad 16$

3. $5,194 \times 33 =$ _____

4. $5,217 \times 18 =$ _____

5. Find the difference between the answer to Number 2 and the answer to Number 3.

Word Problem

6. The park needs a total of 46 new bumper cars, and each bumper car costs $3,200. A factory that makes the bumper cars will buy back 30 of the old cars for $1,400 each. (a) Determine the total cost of purchasing 46 new cars. (b) Calculate the money the park will get for selling 30 of its old cars. (c) If the park uses the money it receives from the old cars to pay for part of the cost of the new cars, how much money will it need to buy the new cars?

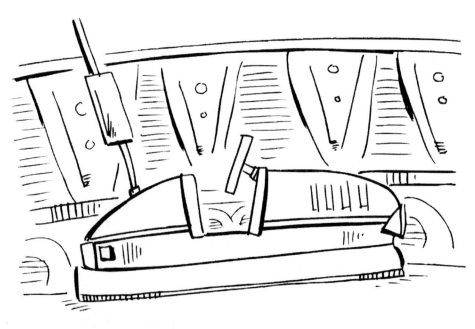

Part III: Division

Workout 49: Division, Subtraction

Find the difference.

1. $24 - 15 - 3 =$ _____

2. $\begin{array}{r} 4{,}600 \\ -\ 3{,}831 \\ \hline \end{array}$

Find the quotient.

3. $8\overline{)48}$

4. $3\overline{)27}$

Word Problem

5. The Modest Lake Town Council has good news. Each member addresses the citizens. The speeches start at 5:28 p.m. and end at 6 p.m. Each of the four members speaks for the same length of time. Determine the length of a time each member speaks.

Workout 50: Division

Find the quotient.

1. $2\overline{)268}$

2. $3\overline{)168}$

3. $3\overline{)681}$

4. $3\overline{)363}$

Word Problem

5. The citizens of Modest Lake jam into the town hall to hear the council members speak. There are so many people that they have to split the people equally into four rooms and watch the speeches on closed circuit TV. If 428 people come to the meeting, how many people are in each room?

Workout 51: Division

Find the quotient.

1. 30)600

2. 5)550

3. 30)3,000

4. 100)20,000

Word Problem

5. Farmer Harrison brings General Thumb to the town meeting. General Thumb is used to speaking to large crowds. The largest crowd he has spoken to had 10,000 people. However, the town council meeting's crowd only numbers 500. How many times bigger than the town council meeting crowd was the largest crowd spoken to by General Thumb?

Name_____ Date:_____

Workout 52: Division

Find the quotient.

1. 3)‾63‾

2. 3)‾51‾

3. 2)‾82‾

4. 6)‾72‾

Word Problem

5. When General Thumb found out that the town's amusement park was in trouble, he jumped at the chance to help. There are 4 months before the park is scheduled to open. General Thumb has 64 great ways to raise money, and the town council wants to use them all. If they use an equal amount of fundraisers each month, how many fundraisers will they use in one month?

Workout 53: Division

Find the quotient.

1. $6\overline{)126}$ **2.** $5\overline{)250}$

3. $7\overline{)287}$ **4.** $4\overline{)164}$

Word Problem

5. During the town meeting, Rosco the Clown entertains the children by making balloon animals. It takes three balloons to make his favorite balloon dog. If Rosco has 153 balloons, how many balloon dogs can he make?

Workout 54: Division

Find the quotient.

1. $7\overline{)147}$

2. $6\overline{)186}$

3. $4\overline{)168}$

4. $4\overline{)328}$

Word Problem

5. The Modest Lake Town Council has enlisted the aid of General Thumb and his friends to help save their amusement park. Minerva the Mysterious and Dr. Chin go over all of the park's debts. There are 336 papers. They sort them into 6 equal piles. How many papers are in each pile?

Name_____ Date:_____

Workout 55: Division

Find the quotient.

1. $2\overline{)1{,}260}$

2. $3\overline{)1{,}170}$

3. $9\overline{)2{,}160}$

4. $4\overline{)2{,}104}$

Word Problem

5. Widow Worthington, the richest person in Modest Lake, is having posters made to help raise money for the amusement park. There are 1,520 posters to be distributed. Eight citizens volunteer to distribute the posters. If the posters are distributed equally among the citizen volunteers, how many posters will each volunteer get?

Name_____ Date:_____

Workout 56: Division, Addition

Find the quotient.

1. $3\overline{)960}$ **2.** $12\overline{)864}$

3. $26\overline{)1,690}$ **4.** $21\overline{)1,134}$

Word Problem

5. The Modest Lake elementary students have made their own fliers to pass out to the public. After handing out 1,183 fliers, the 32 students discovered they still had 257 fliers left to hand out. (a) What was the total number of fliers made? (b) If each student originally received the same amount of fliers, how many fliers did each student start out with?

Workout 57: Division, Multiplication

Find the product.

1. 149
   × 4

2. $187 \times 6 =$ _____

Find the quotient.

3. $10\overline{)520}$

4. $13\overline{)676}$

Word Problem

5. Mr. Gregory and Flying Freda tour the park. In the past 12 years, Freda has traveled to 164 different amusement parks. She has ridden at least six rides at each park. What is the average number of rides she takes in a year?

Workout 58: Division, Interpreting Data

Find the quotient.

1. $18\overline{)954}$

2. $17\overline{)1{,}496}$

3. $21\overline{)2{,}646}$

4. $27\overline{)3{,}321}$

Word Problem

5. General Thumb walks around the park. He counts the number of strides he takes to walk from one end of the park to the other. His stride is exactly 24 inches in length. The park is 2,856 feet across. Determine the number of strides General Thumb takes to cross the park.

Workout 59: Division

Find the quotient.

1. $100\overline{)2{,}000}$

2. $100\overline{)25{,}900}$

3. $200\overline{)22{,}800}$

4. $200\overline{)62{,}800}$

Word Problem

5. Widow Worthington invites Zambul to her charity picnic in the park. She hopes that 200 people will come. She expects the charity picnic to raise $24,600. If each person donates the same amount of money, how much would each individual donate?

Workout 60: Division, Interpreting Data

Find the quotient.

1. $2\overline{)20}$

2. $4\overline{)80}$

3. $3\overline{)60}$

4. $6\overline{)180}$

Word Problem

5. Zambul and Widow Worthington take a boat and row around the lake. The lake is 6 miles around. Their trip around the lake takes an hour and a half. What is the rowboat's average speed per hour?

Part IV: More Multiplication and Division

Workout 61: Multiplication, Division

Find the product.

1.   9
   × 4
   ——

2. $17 \times 5 =$ _____

Find the quotient.

3. $30\overline{)480}$

4. $20\overline{)980}$

Word Problem

5. Rosco the Clown is the world's bumper car racing champion. He rides all day and challenges everyone to race. He has 10 races every hour. He races for 4 hours and competes against the same amount of people each time. He races a total of 960 people. How many people does he race each time?

Workout 62: Multiplication, Division

Find the product.

1. $52 \times 4 =$ _____

2.   676
       $\times$ 4

3.   474
       $\times$ 5

4. Divide the answer to Number 2 by the answer to Number 1.

Word Problem

5. After a hard day of racing, Rosco the Clown is still the bumper car champion. He takes a victory lap in his special mini bumper car. He makes nine laps around the track and travels 500 feet each lap. It takes him 5 minutes to complete all nine laps. Determine how many feet per second his mini car travels.

Name_____ Date:_____

Workout 63: Multiplication, Division

Find the quotient.

1. $400\overline{)1,600}$

2. $200\overline{)1,800}$

3. $700\overline{)2,100}$

4. $600\overline{)2,400}$

Word Problem

5. Flying Freda is going to attempt the world record distance for the human cannonball. She needs to fly 1,800 feet to break the record. She needs one pound of cannon powder for every 100 yards she wants to travel. How many pounds does she need to break the record?

Workout 64: Multiplication, Division, Addition

Find the sum.

1. $1,200 + 400 =$ _____

2. $1,600 + 300 =$ _____

3. $1,500 + 800 =$ _____

4. Divide the answer to Number 1 by 40.

Word Problem

5. A target has been placed on a barge in the middle of Modest Lake. It is floating 1,600 feet away from shore. Flying Freda's cannon is 200 feet back from the edge of the lake. When the cannon fires, Freda will fly for 3 seconds and then hit the target. How many yards per second does she travel?

Workout 65: Division

Find the quotient.

1. 7)2,128

2. 6)2,448

3. 8)2,448

4. 3)2,448

Word Problem

5. The Grand Hall's paint has faded from its once brilliant blue and yellow to dull shades of its former colors. Mr. Gregory is leading the crew of painters who are bringing the hall back to its glory. They use 184 containers of paint. Each container is equal to ⅛ gallon of paint. How many gallons of paint did they use?

Workout 66: Multiplication, Division

Find the quotient.

1. $624 \div 4 =$ _____

2. $560 \div 8 =$ _____

3. $180 \div 12 =$ _____

4. $235 \div 5 =$ _____

Word Problem

5. To finish painting the Grand Hall, Mr. Gregory needs to order more paint. The local hardware store has agreed to sell Mr. Gregory the paint at a price of $8 per quart. He spends $576 for all of the new paint. (a) Determine how many quarts of paint he bought. (b) How many gallons did he purchase?

Workout 67: Division

Find the quotient.

1. $1,092 \div 14 =$ _____

2. $1,008 \div 21 =$ _____

3. $2,294 \div 62 =$ _____

4. $1,029 \div 21 =$ _____

Word Problem

5. Ma Harrison is finally going to open a bakery. The park will be an excellent location. Her shop will be at the park entrance, next to the gift shop. The gift shop is four times large than the bakery. If the gift shop has an area of 3,456 square feet, what is the area of Ma's Bakery?

Workout 68: Division, Subtraction

Find the quotient.

1. $1,008 \div 84 =$ _____

2. $1,650 \div 55 =$ _____

3. $441 \div 21 =$ _____

4. $2,560 \div 8 =$ _____

Word Problem

5. Ma Harrison's apple-strawberry pie has won the county fair for the past 5 years. For the grand opening of her new bakery, Ma will bake 360 total pies. If 1 out of every 3 of the pies in the bakery are apple-strawberry, how many pies make up the remaining pies?

Workout 69: Division, Addition, Units of Measure

Convert from inches to feet.

1. 96 inches = _____ feet

2. 624 inches = _____ feet

Convert from inches to yards.

3. 144 inches = _____ yards

4. 468 inches = _____ yards

Word Problem

5. Widow Worthington is buying material to make new drapes for the park's hotel. She buys 648 inches of gold fabric, 540 inches of red fabric, and 252 inches of dark red fabric. What is the total number of yards of fabric she purchased?

Workout 70: Division, Time

Convert from minutes to hours.

1. 240 minutes = _____ hours

2. 120 minutes = _____ hours

3. 600 minutes = _____ hours

4. 840 minutes = _____ hours

Word Problem

5. Minerva is quite a seamstress. She helps Widow Worthington make the drapes for the hotel windows. It takes her 540 minutes to make 12 sets of drapes. How many hours did it take her to make the 12 drapes?

Workout 71: Multiplication, Division, Multiple Operations

Solve the problems below using multiplication, division, addition, and subtraction.

1. $(22 \times 3) - 8 =$ _____

2. $(28 \times 2) - 12 =$ _____

3. $(32 \div 4) + 7 =$ _____

4. $(45 \div 15) + 19 =$ _____

Word Problem

5. A group of 96 volunteers gather at the park to help with cleanup duties. General Thumb is in charge of job assignments. He divides the volunteers into 12 equal groups. One of the groups is assigned to clean up under the roller coaster. Each of the members of the roller coaster clean-up group gets three garbage bags. The whole group uses all but three of the bags. Determine the total number of garbage bags the group used.

Workout 72: Multiplication, Division, Multiple Operations

Solve the problems below using multiplication, division, addition, and subtraction.

1. $(47 \times 5) - 21 =$ _____

2. $(59 \times 12) - 35 =$ _____

3. $(156 \div 4) + 18 =$ _____

4. $(321 \div 3) + 89 =$ _____

Word Problem

5. Zambul has been given the assignment to set up the cars on the roller coaster. He works a total of 42 hours during the course of 4 days. He worked for 6 hours on the first day, and the next 3 days, he worked an equal amount of hours each day. How many hours did he work each of the last 3 days?

Workout 73: Multiplication, Division, Multiple Operations

Solve the problems below using multiplication, division, addition, and subtraction.

1. $(81 \div 3) + 15 =$ _____

2. $(169 \div 13) + 8 =$ _____

3. $(213 \times 6) - 25 =$ _____

4. $(114 \times 9) - 76 =$ _____

Word Problem

5. Zambul is assembling the cars for the roller coaster. So far, the roller coaster train has 11 cars. Zambul connects one more car to the roller coaster train. The train is now 98 feet in length. The front car is 2 feet longer than the rest of the cars. All the other cars are the same length. What is the length of the last car?

Workout 74: Multiplication, Division, Multiple Operations

Find the product.

1. $5 \times 6 \times 7 =$ _____

2. $10 \times 10 \times 10 \times 10 =$ _____

Solve the problems below using multiplication and division.

3. $\left(48 \times 3\right) \div 6 =$ _____

4. $\left(54 \times 3\right) \div 9 =$ _____

Word Problem

5. Minerva the Mysterious has a new magic trick called "The Disappearing Cow." She needs a large piece of cloth to drape over a cow, so she sews four pieces of cloth together to make the size she needs. Two of the pieces of cloth are each 45 inches long, another cloth is 54 inches long, and the last cloth is 60 inches long. What is the total length in feet of all four pieces of cloth?

Workout 75: Multiplication, Division, Multiple Operations

Solve the problems below using division, addition, and subtraction.

1. $(56 \div 8) + 12 =$ _____

2. $(54 \div 6) + 17 =$ _____

3. $(81 \div 27) + 13 =$ _____

4. $(625 \div 25) - 10 =$ _____

Word Problem

5. Many of the townsfolk of Modest Lake want to help fix up their amusement park. Dr. Chin makes up eight lists of volunteers and their job assignments. There are a total of 372 volunteers. The number of volunteers on seven of the lists is the same. There are four more people on the eighth list than on the other lists. How many people are on the eighth list?

Workout 76: Division, Multiple Operations

Solve the problems below using division, addition, and subtraction.

1. $\left(125 \div 25\right) - 5 = $ _____

2. $\left(256 \div 16\right) - 5 = $ _____

3. $\left(121 \div 11\right) - 10 = $ _____

4. $\left(196 \div 14\right) - 13 = $ _____

Word Problem

5. All around the park are streamers of multicolored pennants. A car dealership has donated a set of new streamers, and Flying Freda is climbing the poles around the park to hang up the streamers. A single streamer has 42 pennants. One out of every seven of the pennants is blue. How many blue pennants are there?

Workout 77: Multiplication, Division, Units of Measure

Solve the problems below using division and multiplication.

1. $(35 \div 7) \times 8 =$ _____

2. $(72 \div 9) \times 3 =$ _____

3. $(51 \div 3) \times 8 =$ _____

4. $(63 \div 7) \times 11 =$ _____

Word Problem

5. Widow Worthington owns a carpet warehouse. She is donating four new carpets for the Grand Hall. Each carpet is 12 yards long. The total cost of the carpets is $2,880. What is the unit price for one foot of carpet?

Workout 78: Multiplication, Division, Multiple Operations

Solve the problems below using multiplication, division, addition, and subtraction.

1. $(15 \times 5) - 8 =$ _____

2. $(95 \div 19) + 42 =$ _____

3. $(400 \div 16) - 10 =$ _____

4. $(343 \div 49) - 2 =$ _____

Word Problem

5. Rosco the Clown loves miniature golf. He is fixing up the park's mini golf course and plans to call it "Clown Around Golf." There are 18 different golf challenges. Water is used as a challenge in one out of every six of the holes. One out of every three of the holes has some type of wooden barrier. The remaining holes have moving challenges. How many holes have moving challenges?

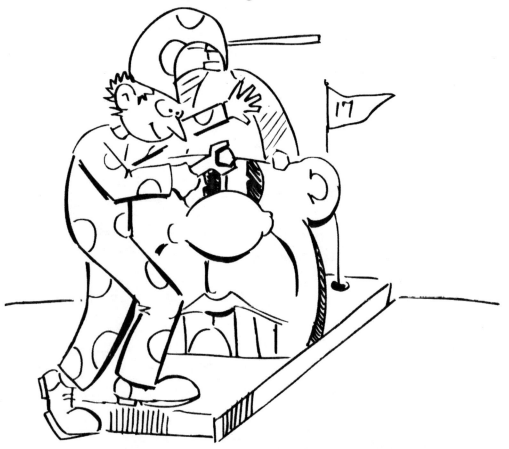

Workout 79: Multiplication, Division, Addition

Solve the problems below using multiplication and addition.

1. $(2 \times 12) + (2 \times 10) =$ _____

2. $(2 \times 25) + (2 \times 40) =$ _____

Find the product.

3. $10,000 \times 100 =$ _____

4. $7 \times 7 \times 7 \times 7 =$ _____

Word Problem

5. Rosco is using rope to enclose the perimeter of his golf course. The course is located inside a rectangular-shaped area (see Figure 2 below). He is going to attach the rope to poles spaced 4 feet apart. How many poles will he need to enclose the entire perimeter of the golf course?

Miniature Golf Course   20 Feet

24 Feet

Workout 80: Division

Solve the problems below using multiplication and division.

1. $1{,}134 \div 27 = $ _____

2. $625 \times 25 = $ _____

3. $10{,}000 \div 100 = $ _____

4. $5 \times 7 \times 5 \times 7 = $ _____

Word Problem

5. The Fun House needs its entrance lights replaced. There are 90 light bulbs in the front entrance. Rosco the Clown has just replaced five out of every six of them. How many light bulbs still need to be replaced?

Part V: Fractions

Workout 81: Fractions

Reduce each fraction below to its simplest form.

1. $\dfrac{2}{6}$ _____

2. $\dfrac{5}{10}$ _____

3. $\dfrac{16}{20}$ _____

4. $\dfrac{9}{12}$ _____

Word Problem

5. General Thumb loves the all of the rides at the amusement park. He spends 8 hours riding one day. He rides the Paratrooper for 2 hours. Write a fraction representing the amount of time he spends riding the Paratrooper during this particular day.

Workout 82: Fractions

Compare the fractions using < or >.

1. $\dfrac{1}{2}$ ◯ $\dfrac{2}{8}$
          2. $\dfrac{5}{6}$ ◯ $\dfrac{2}{3}$

3. $\dfrac{7}{10}$ ◯ $\dfrac{4}{5}$
          4. $\dfrac{8}{9}$ ◯ $\dfrac{5}{6}$

Word Problem

5. It is time to prepare for the park's grand opening. General Thumb needs to conduct a last-minute check of all of the parts of the park. Flying Freda reports that four of the stands need some type of repairs. There are 20 stands. Write a fraction in simplest form to represent the number of stands that need repair out of the total number of stands.

Workout 83: Fractions, Addition

Find the sum.

1. $\dfrac{1}{3} + \dfrac{1}{3} =$ _____

2. $\dfrac{1}{4} + \dfrac{2}{4} =$ _____

3. $\dfrac{3}{10} + \dfrac{4}{10} =$ _____

4. $\dfrac{1}{8} + \dfrac{7}{8}$ _____

Word Problem

5. Freda makes ⅜ of the cotton candy treats with blue color. She makes ⅖ of the cotton candy treats with purple color. She makes the rest of the cotton candy treats pink. (a) What fractional part of the cotton candy treats are blue and purple? (b) What fractional part of the candy treats are pink?

Workout 84: Fractions

Solve to find the fractional parts of each number.

1. What is $\frac{1}{3}$ of 21? _____

2. What is $\frac{1}{4}$ of 24? _____

3. What is $\frac{1}{5}$ of 40? _____

4. What is $\frac{1}{6}$ of 42? _____

Word Problem

5. Rosco the Clown is setting up a duck pond game. There are 300 ducks in the game. Each duck wins a prize, but ⅙ of the ducks win a stuffed dog for a prize. How many ducks have a stuffed dog as a prize?

Name_____ Date:_____

Workout 85: Fractions

Reduce each fraction below to its simplest form.

1. $\frac{18}{21}$ _____

2. $\frac{15}{25}$ _____

3. $\frac{21}{35}$ _____

4. $\frac{16}{24}$ _____

Word Problem

5. The Grand Park Hotel is preparing for the park's reopening. The maids dust each of the 114 rooms in the hotel. Each maid dusts ⅙ of the total number of rooms. How many rooms does each maid dust?

Workout 86: Fractions, Addition

Find the sum.

1. $\dfrac{1}{2} + \dfrac{1}{2} =$ _____

2. $\dfrac{1}{4} + \dfrac{1}{4} =$ _____

3. $\dfrac{1}{6} + \dfrac{3}{6} =$ _____

4. $\dfrac{4}{8} + \dfrac{4}{8} =$ _____

Word Problem

5. Widow Worthington counts the linens on each floor of the hotel. The first floor has ¼ of the hotel's linens. The second floor has ⁵⁄₁₂ of the hotel's linens and the third floor has ⅙ of the hotel's linens. What fractional part of the hotel's total linens are on the fourth floor? Simplify your answer.

Workout 87: Fractions, Addition

Create a fraction using the numbers below and reduce it to its simplest form.

1. 30 out of 45 _____

2. 20 out of 100 _____

Find the sum.

3. $\dfrac{2}{5} + \dfrac{2}{5} =$ _____

4. $1\frac{1}{8} + 2\frac{4}{8} =$ _____

Word Problem

5. Zambul is attaching all the newly painted animals to the carousel ride. He has 120 bolts. Each animal needs 10 bolts. What fraction of the total number of the bolts is used to attach each animal? Simplify your answer.

Workout 88: Fractions, Addition

Convert each improper fraction into a mixed number.

1. $\frac{14}{3}$ _____

2. $\frac{24}{9}$ _____

3. $\frac{15}{2}$ _____

4. $\frac{27}{4}$ _____

Word Problem

5. Zambul is building the park's stages. He nails a ⅝-inch thick piece of wood to a ⅞-inch thick piece of wood to make the floor of the stage. How thick is the stage floor. Write your answer as a mixed number in simplest form.

Workout 89: Fractions, Subtraction

Find the difference.

1. $5\frac{5}{6} - 2\frac{3}{6} =$ _____

2. $7\frac{5}{8} - 4\frac{3}{8} =$ _____

3. $11\frac{9}{10} - 9\frac{4}{10} =$ _____

4. $3\frac{20}{21} - 1\frac{17}{21} =$ _____

Word Problem

5. Farmer Harrison buys the bags of potatoes to make the park's famous fries. One bag weighs 80 $\frac{13}{16}$ pounds. Another bag weighs 78 $\frac{5}{16}$ pounds. What is the difference between the weight of the bags?

Workout 90: Fractions, Addition, Subtraction, Time

Find the sum.

1. $\dfrac{1}{2}+\dfrac{1}{2}+\dfrac{1}{2}+\dfrac{1}{2}=$ _____

2. $\dfrac{5}{8}+\dfrac{3}{8}+\dfrac{2}{8}+\dfrac{6}{8}=$ _____

Find the difference.

3. $\dfrac{11}{2}-\dfrac{9}{2}=$ _____

4. $7-\frac{1}{2}=$ _____

Word Problem

5. Potatoes will be cut into fries by a local manufacturer for the park's concession stands. The company has a process that cuts ½ pound of potatoes every 30 seconds. How many minutes will it take the company to cut 80 pounds of potatoes?

Workout 91: Fractions, Addition, Subtraction

Find the sum.

1. $\dfrac{1}{6} + \dfrac{1}{3} =$ _____

2. $\dfrac{7}{10} + \dfrac{1}{5} =$ _____

Find the difference.

3. $\dfrac{7}{8} - \dfrac{1}{4} =$ _____

4. $\dfrac{1}{3} - \dfrac{2}{9} =$ _____

Word Problem

5. Minerva the Mysterious operates the Wheel of Fortune. There are 252 spaces on the wheel, which is made up of 14 different colors. $\frac{5}{14}$ of the spaces are blue and $\frac{2}{7}$ of the spaces are red. What is the difference between the blue and red spaces?

Workout 92: Fractions, Addition, Subtraction

Find the difference.

1. $1 - \frac{3}{4} =$ _____

2. $1 - \frac{4}{5} =$ _____

Find the sum.

3. $\frac{3}{8} + \frac{7}{8} =$ _____

4. $4\frac{1}{2} + \frac{2}{3} =$ _____

Word Problem

5. The midway of the amusement park is lined with games and concession stands. One of the games is Balloon Pop. It takes ¾ of a bag of balloons to fill the entire game board. How many bags will it take to fill the board 8 times?

Workout 93: Fractions, Subtraction

Find the difference.

1. $2\frac{1}{2} - \frac{2}{5} =$ _____

2. $\frac{7}{8} - \frac{3}{4} =$ _____

3. $2\frac{7}{8} - 2\frac{2}{3} =$ _____

4. $\frac{3}{4} - \frac{9}{16} =$ _____

Word Problem

5. Dr. Chin has purchased rolls of ride tickets for the park. He passes out 18 ¾ rolls of tickets. Of those rolls, he gives the booth at Kiddy Land 3 ½ rolls of tickets. How many rolls of tickets does he have left?

Workout 94: Fractions, Addition

Find the sum.

1. $19\frac{7}{8} + 6\frac{5}{16} =$ _____

2. $2\frac{1}{2} + \frac{2}{3} =$ _____

3. $\frac{5}{18} + 2\frac{5}{6} =$ _____

4. $\frac{5}{8} + 2\frac{1}{3} =$ _____

Word Problem

5. The ticket booths at the park are ready for business. Dr. Chin made the hole in the window 4 ⅜ inches wider to make it easier to collect money and pass out tickets. The original hole was 5 ½ inches wide. How wide is the new window hole?

Name_____ Date:_____

Workout 95: Fractions, Addition, Subtraction

Solve each problem using addition or subtraction.

1. $6\frac{1}{8} + 2\frac{1}{3} =$ _____

2. $6\frac{3}{8} - 2\frac{1}{3} =$ _____

3. $4\frac{1}{2} - 4\frac{5}{12} =$ _____

4. $8\frac{1}{2} + 4\frac{7}{12} =$ _____

Word Problem

5. The members of the middle school chorus arrive to fold coupon flyers. There are $4\frac{11}{12}$ boxes of fliers. When the chorus leaves, there are $1\frac{5}{6}$ boxes left to fold. How many boxes of fliers did the chorus members fold?

Workout 96: Fractions, Addition, Subtraction

Find the sum.

1. $\frac{1}{2} + 1 + \frac{1}{2} + 1 =$ _____

2. $\frac{2}{3} + 1\frac{1}{3} + \frac{2}{3} + 1\frac{1}{3} =$ _____

3. $1\frac{4}{8} + 1\frac{3}{8} =$ _____

4. $\frac{1}{4} + \frac{1}{8} + \frac{1}{3} =$ _____

Word Problem

5. Flying Freda's favorite treat is candy apples. She places the apples on a tray. Each apple about is about 3 ½ inches wide. Freda sets the apples about ¾ of an inch apart from each other and the edge of the tray. How wide is a tray that can hold three apples in a row?

Workout 97: Fractions, Subtraction

Find the difference.

1. $2\frac{1}{2} - 1\frac{11}{12} =$ _____

2. $6\frac{2}{10} - 4\frac{3}{5} =$ _____

3. $8\frac{2}{3} - 4\frac{5}{6} =$ _____

4. $7\frac{3}{16} - 2\frac{7}{8} =$ _____

Word Problem

5. Rosco the Clown is filling balloons with helium for the opening day of the Modest Lake Amusement Park. He has 5 ¼ tanks of helium. He uses 3 ¹³⁄₁₆ tanks to fill all the balloons. How many tanks of helium are left?

Workout 98: Fractions, Time

Convert from minutes to hours. Reduce any fractions to their simplest forms.

1. 120 minutes = _____ hours

2. 150 minutes = _____ hours

3. 200 minutes = _____ hours

4. 525 minutes = _____ hours

Word Problem

5. On the park's opening day, Rosco gives away free helium balloons. He tries to give a balloon to every child he meets. Rosco spends 345 minutes giving balloons away to children. How many hours does he spend handing out balloons? Reduce any fractions to their simplest forms.

Workout 99: Fractions, Time

Convert from hours to minutes. Reduce any fractions to their simplest forms.

1. $1\frac{1}{2}$ hours = _____ minutes

2. $3\frac{3}{10}$ hours = _____ minutes

3. $2\frac{1}{6}$ hours = _____ minutes

4. $5\frac{2}{3}$ hours = _____ minutes

Word Problem

5. General Thumb welcomes the visitors to the park. He announces the attractions and the location of events. It takes him 3 minutes to make his announcement. If he repeats the announcement nonstop for an hour and a half, how many times does he repeat the welcome announcement?

Name_____ Date:_____

Workout 100: Fractions, Addition, Units of Measure

Find the sum.

1. $3\frac{1}{2}$ ft. $+ 1\frac{5}{8}$ ft.= _____

2. $8\frac{1}{12} + 4\frac{5}{6} =$ _____

3. $4\frac{7}{8} + 2\frac{1}{12} =$ _____

4. $12\frac{9}{16} + 4\frac{1}{2} =$ _____

Word Problem

5. General Thumb has Zambul hold him up so he can see the huge opening day crowd. Zambul is 6 ½ feet tall. When Zambul raises his arms straight up he can reach another 2 ⅔ feet above his head. Including his hat, General Thumb is 4 ½ feet tall. If Zambul's arms are raised straight up while holding General Thumb, what is the total distance from the top of General Thumb's hat to the ground?

Part VI: Decimals

Workout 101: Decimals, Addition, Money

Find the sum.

1. $12.1 + 3.4 =$ _____

2.   29.4
     $+\ 4.7$

3. $\$14.98 + \$11.56 =$ _____

4. $\$36.19$
     $+\ \$23.47$

Word Problem

5. Widow Worthington is quite pleased with the Grand Hotel's reopening. All of the rooms in the hotel have been rented for opening night. A room costs $123.67 for one night. There is an additional tax of $23.12 on the room. What is the total cost of a room for one night?

Workout 102: Decimals, Addition, Money

Find the sum.

1. $64 + 2.5 =$ _____

2. $4.8 + 300 =$ _____

3. $\$89.12 + \$22.36 =$ _____

4. $78.5 + 9.09 =$ _____

Word Problem

5. Dr. Chin and Minerva had their tuxedos cleaned and pressed for the grand opening of the park. It cost Dr. Chin $32.56 to get his tux cleaned. Minerva paid $26.78 for her cleaning. What was the total cost to get both tuxedos cleaned?

Workout 103: Decimals, Addition, Money

Find the sum.

1. 12,564.09
      + 7,225.12

2. $19.56 + 8.23 =$ _____

3. $12.87
       + $18.65

4. $17.60 + 13.25 =$ _____

Word Problem

5. Opening day business for the park is outstanding. In the first 15 minutes, the park makes $6,235.25. In the next 45 minutes, the park makes $18,789.45. How much did the park make in the first hour it was open?

Name_____ Date:_____

Workout 104: Decimals, Addition, Units of Measure

Find the sum.

1. $1.025 + 0.096 =$ _____

2. $67.04 + 1.9612 =$ _____

3. $40.028 + 3.207 =$ _____

4. $789.8 + 0.52 =$ _____

Word Problem

5. It has always been one of Farmer Harrison's dreams to be the engineer on the park train, and he has finally gotten his chance. The train is a replica of town's first steam locomotive. The miniature train engine is 2.857 meters long. The miniature coal car is 1.625 meters long. Determine the length in meters of the coal car and the engine combined.

Workout 105: Decimals, Addition, Units of Measure

Compare the decimal numbers using < or >.

1. 89.7 ◯ 89.07

2. 15.151 ◯ 15.155

Find the sum.

3. $2.3 + 8.2 + 3.6 =$ _____

4. $2.2 + 7 + 3.7 + 4.13 =$ _____

Word Problem

5. The train has 12 passenger cars. Each car can seat four people. The maximum weight a single car can hold is 145.9 kg. If four passengers weigh 23.5 kg, 26.86 kg, 31.04 kg, and 42.78 kg, can the car safely hold all of their weight?

Name_____ Date:_____

Workout 106: Decimals, Subtraction, Units of Measure

Find the difference.

1. $4 - 2.14 =$ _____

2. $16 - 11.5 =$ _____

3.   17.48
       $- 5.29$
       ‾‾‾‾‾‾‾

4.   21.789
       $- 18.784$
       ‾‾‾‾‾‾‾‾

Word Problem

5. The carousel is a popular ride. Minerva always rides on her favorite llama. The llama is set on a pole measuring 4 meters in length. From the tip of the llama's toes to the top of its head measures 2.565 meters. What is the difference between the llama's height and the length of the pole?

Workout 107: Decimals, Subtraction, Money

Find the difference.

1. $1300.00
 − $47.17

2. $150.406 - 38.477 = $ _____

3. $908.56 - 873.68 = $ _____

4. $9 - 4.224 = $ _____

Word Problem

5. Flying Freda is going to put on an air show for the Modest Lake Amusement Park's opening day. The budget for entertainment for the opening day is $923. The pilot of the plane is charging $327.49 for the use of the plane for the entire day. How much is leftover in the day's entertainment budget after paying for the plane?

Name_____ Date:_____

Workout 108: Decimals, Multiplication, Units of Measure

Find the product.

1. 1.15
  × 2
  ____

2. 8.897
  × 10
  ____

3. $46.2251 \times 2 =$ _____

4. $66.51 \times 12 =$ _____

Word Problem

5. Freda performs her most daring trick during the opening day air show. She hangs from the airplane by a rope using only one hand. To help her hold on to the rope she has tied three knots. There is a distance of 21.63 cm between the top knot and the bottom knot, and the middle knot is 12.46 cm above the bottom knot. How much distance is between the middle knot and the top knot?

Workout 109: Decimals, Multiplication, Money

Find the product.

1. 6.17
    × 2.2

2. 8.533
    × 1.3

3. $1.2 \times 2 =$ _____

4. $21.125 \times 5 =$ _____

Word Problem

5. One of opening day's big events is the pie-eating contest. The winner of the contest will receive a gift certificate valued at $35.50 and two all-day ride passes valued at $19.34 each. If the pies were donated to the park by Ma Harrison and the budget for the contest is $100, how much money is left in the budget after paying for the prizes?

Workout 110: Decimals, Multiple Operations, Money

Solve the problems below using addition and subtraction.

1. $38.33 + 14.56 - 23.67 =$ _____

2. $\$22.60 + \$53.00 - \$42.78 =$ _____

3. $276.00 + 12.1 - 4.327 =$ _____

4. $334.00 + 199.783 - 78.586 =$ _____

Word Problem

5. Business is booming at Ma Harrison's pie shop. By 3 p.m. on opening day, Ma has sold all of her pies and has made $316.10. The ingredients to make the pies cost $98.12, and she paid her help a total of $56.73. After she pays for the cost of making the pie, including the cost to pay her help, what was her profit?

Workout 111: Decimals, Multiplication, Division

Find the product.

1. 1,385
   × 1.24
   —————

2. 1,268
   × 1.38
   —————

Find the quotient.

3. 3)‾3.762‾

4. 5)‾9.735‾

Word Problem

5. It is the greatest opening day in the park's history. All of the rides and attractions are a success! The Ferris Wheel is the last ride to close on opening day. It takes four tickets to ride the Ferris Wheel, and each ticket costs 45 cents. There are a total of 4,920 tickets in the Ferris Wheel's ticket collection box. (a) How many people rode the Ferris Wheel? (b) How much money did the ride make?

Workout 112: Decimals, Division, Money

Find the quotient. Round to the nearest whole number.

1. $1,253 \overline{)62,381}$

2. $6,539 \overline{)92,716}$

Find the quotient. Round to the nearest cent.

3. $10,627 \overline{)\$117,638}$

4. $11,412 \overline{)\$125,073}$

Word Problem

5. At the end of the day, the town council and General Thumb total the day's cash. The park brought in $170,835, and there were 32,540 people counted entering the park. Find the average amount of money spent by each person.

Name_____ Date:_____

Workout 113: Decimals, Division

Find the quotient. Round to the nearest cent.

1. $15 ÷ 6 =$ _____

2. $44 ÷ 7 =$ _____

3. $8\overline{)\$65}$

4. $3\overline{)\$58}$

Word Problem

5. The amusement park offers special birthday party events. The party event includes a cake, ice cream, party favors, and a performance from Rosco the Clown. The party costs $45 for 12 children. How much does it cost per child?

Name_____ Date:_____

Workout 114: Decimals, Multiplication, Subtraction, Money

Find the product.

1. $15 \times 0.10 =$ _____

2.
$$\begin{array}{r} 1.8 \\ \times 1.3 \\ \hline \end{array}$$

Find the difference.
3.
$$\begin{array}{r} \$123.00 \\ -\$118.30 \\ \hline \end{array}$$

4. $\$164.50 - \$125.61 =$ _____

Word Problem

5. Rosco the Clown gives every child that attends a birthday event at the park a 10% discount coupon for a full day of rides. The full-day ride pass costs $13. If 12 children use the coupon, what is the total amount of money that will be saved?

Workout 115: Decimals, Rounding, Money

Round the numbers below to the greatest possible place value.

1. $6.54 _____

2. 2,351.23 _____

3. 5,642.912 _____

4. Multiply the answer to Number 1 by the answer to Number 2.

Word Problem

5. The amusement park buys all the apples it can from local growers to make its candy apples. To be fair, Farmer Harrison helps set a standard price for every bushel of apples. The park pays $8.75 for each bushel. Estimate the total cost for 1,478 bushels.

Workout 116: Decimals, Multiplication, Money

Find the product.

1. $1.62
   $\times\quad 6$

2. $5.62 \times 4 \times 3 =$ _____

3. $6.20
   $\times\ 3.2$

4. $9.34 \times 5.1 =$ _____

Word Problem

5. Farmer Harrison's dairy cattle provide the milk that is used to make ice cream for the amusement park's concession stands. The milk from each cow has an average daily value of $8.36. What is total value for the milk from 12 cows for 5 days?

Workout 117: Decimals, Multiplication

Find the product.

1. $360 \times 0.4 =$ _____

2. $240 \times 0.375 =$ _____

3. $420 \times 0.571 =$ _____

4. $640 \times 0.75 =$ _____

Word Problem

5. The pies from Ma Harrison's bakeshop are the newest sensation. Minerva the Mysterious helps Ma set up a Web site to sell her pies over the Internet. Ma sells 540 pies a week, and 0.30 of those sales come from the Internet. How many pies does she sell over the Internet?

Workout 118: Decimals, Multiplication, Addition, Money

Find the product.

1.
$$\begin{array}{r} 73 \\ \times\, 0.5 \\ \hline \end{array}$$

2. $0.6 \times 0.6 =$ _____

Find the sum.

3.
$$\begin{array}{r} \$3.40 \\ +\, \$5.00 \\ \hline \end{array}$$

4. $\$9.41 + \$7.23 =$ _____

Word Problem

5. The pies from Ma Harrison's pie shop are shipped all over the country. The delivery company charges $5.60 plus $.80 for every half a pound a package weights. The pie packages weigh 2.5 pounds each. How much does it cost to ship a single pie?

Workout 119: Decimals, Division, Time

Find the quotient.

1. $0.7\overline{)14}$

2. $0.4\overline{)3.2}$

3. $0.6\overline{)24.12}$

4. $1.2\overline{)1.224}$

Word Problem

5. A national television network is doing a story on the amusement park's amazing recovery and success. Because General Thumb is so interesting, his interview lasts 0.6 of an hour. The network will divide the interview into four equal parts. How many minutes is each part?

Workout 120: Decimals, Division, Time

Find the quotient.

1. $0.9\overline{)18}$

2. $1.6\overline{)3.2}$

3. $0.09\overline{)3.627}$

4. $0.04\overline{)1.12}$

Word Problem

5. The Modest Lake Amusement Park story is so popular that the television network runs a series of reports on the continuing success of the park. The update is 0.05 hours long. The entire news program is 0.75 hours long. How many times longer is the entire news program than the segment?

Part VII: Mixed Practice for Math Review

Workout 121: Division, Money

Find the quotient.

1. $4\overline{)16,000}$

2. $2\overline{)84,000}$

3. $6\overline{)660,000}$

4. $7\overline{)3,500,000}$

Word Problem

5. Dr. Chin has contacted a group of medical professionals. They are planning to invest in a luxury housing development in Modest Lake, due to the town's revitalization. The development will cost $4.8 million. If each of the six investors contributes an equal amount, how much will each investor contribute?

Workout 122: Division, Fractions

Find the quotient.

1. $15 \div \frac{1}{3} =$ _____

2. $21 \div \frac{3}{7} =$ _____

3. $\frac{3}{5} \overline{)45}$

4. $\frac{2}{6} \overline{)36}$

Word Problem

5. The construction of the new housing development is progressing at a fast pace. In 23 days, one quarter of the project is complete. If the housing project continues at this pace, how long will it take to be completed?

Workout 123: Multiplication, Money

Find the product.

1. $\$120 \times 14 =$ _____

2. $\$135 \times 18 =$ _____

3. $\begin{array}{r} \$142 \\ \times \quad 12 \\ \hline \end{array}$

4. $\begin{array}{r} \$168 \\ \times \quad 25 \\ \hline \end{array}$

Word Problem

5. The Modest Lake Hotel is offering a family special of $155 for an entire weekend. Thirty-three families take advantage of the special. How much money did the hotel make from this promotion?

Workout 124: Subtraction, Multiplication, Money

Find the product.

1. $3.40
  $\times\ \ 6$

2. $6.50 \times 8 =$ _____

Find the difference.

3. $125.30
  $- \$35.00$

4. $165.90 - \$65.00 =$ _____

Word Problem

5. The bellhops at the hotel work for $5.50 an hour plus tips. One bellhop made $134.50 for an eight-hour shift. How much did he make in tips?

Name_____ Date:_____

Workout 125: Addition, Division, Averages

Find the averages for the following lists of numbers.

1. 95, 63, 82, and 74 _____

2. 62, 41, 86, 54, and 71_____

3. 74, 110, 96, and 53 _____

4. 112, 129, 94, 87, and 106 _____

Word Problem

5. Flying Freda performs the human cannonball trick five times each day. She flies 122, 124, 126, 118, and 130 feet during one day's performances. What is the average length of her flight?

Workout 126: Addition, Multiplication, Interpreting Data

Find the sum.

1. $62.00
$54.00
+ $27.00

2. $73 + $68 + $92 = _____

Find the product.

3. $74
× 5

4. $86 × 7 = _____

Word Problem

5. Freda expands her performances to include water skiing and aerial stunts. She hires a pilot, a boat driver, and six skiers. They perform three times each day. Use the chart below to determine the total daily cost of the performers' salaries.

Job Description	Wage for Each Performance
Pilot	$75
Driver	$35
Skier	$24

Name_____ Date:_____

Workout 127: Subtraction, Multiplication, Division

Find the product.

1. 110
   × 22
   _____

2. $132 \times 30 =$ _____

Find the difference.

3. 3,521
   − 1,598
   _____

4. $5,937 - 3,699 =$ _____

Word Problem

5. Zambul the Strongman challenges everyone to compete in a test of strength. His favorite competition is the block race. Each contestant tries to carry a 400-pound block as fast as he or she can for 40 feet. Zambul wins every race this season. He has raced twice a day, 6 days a week, for 9 weeks. A mile is 5,280 feet. How many more races must Zambul compete in to have run a mile?

Workout 128: Interpreting Data

Order the numbers below from least to greatest.

1. 16, 34, 10, and 24 _____   **2.** 64, 52, 71, and 98 _____

Order the numbers below from greatest to least.

3. 123, 94, 110, and 130 _____   **4.** 85, 75, 96, and 98_____

Word Problem

5. Mr. Gregory and his son come every weekend to the park. Use the chart below to make a bar graph of how many times they have ridden each ride.

Ride Name	Times Ridden
Roto Planes	32
Starship	40
Roller Coaster	26
Ferris Wheel	28

Name_____ Date:_____

Workout 129: Multiplication, Fractions, Time

Find the product.

1. $45 \times \frac{4}{5} =$ _____

2. $63 \times \frac{2}{9} =$ _____

3. $56 \times \frac{3}{7} =$ _____

4. $84 \times \frac{2}{3} =$ _____

Word Problem

5. General Thumb and Minerva take a tour of the amusement park at one of its busiest times. The crowds of visitors make driving in their cart difficult. It takes 45 minutes to get from the front entrance to the rear exit of the park. When the park is empty a cart can be driven that distance in $\frac{2}{15}$ of the time. How long does it take travel that distance when the park is empty?

Workout 130: Multiplication, Fractions, Money

Find the product.

1. $16,000 \times \frac{2}{4} =$ _____

2. $18,000 \times \frac{4}{6} =$ _____

3. $25,000 \times \frac{6}{10} =$ _____

4. $5,000 \times \frac{5}{8} =$ _____

Word Problem

5. The park makes $32,000 in one weekend. To pay off its debt, ⅜ of the money is put into a special account. How much money is left after the deposit into the special account is made?

Answer Key

Part I: Addition and Subtraction

Workout 1
1. 89
2. 708
3. 399
4. 1,066
5. $1,246

Workout 2
1. 2,729
2. 5,090
3. 3,048
4. 4,698
5. 5,090
6. $7,967

Workout 3
1. 98, 121, 156, 179, 184
2. 698, 703, 724, 749, 754
3. >
4. <
5. (a) $475; (b) Zambul; (c) Minerva; (d) $21

Workout 4
1. $104
2. $629
3. $565
4. $168
5. $3

Workout 5
1. $3,228
2. $5,447
3. $264
4. $2,246
5. (a) $52,448; (b) 2001

Workout 6
1. 1,642
2. 2,830
3. 4,654
4. 9,129
5. 9,129
6. (a) $141,690; (b) 2002; (c) 2001

Workout 7
1. <
2. <
3. <
4. <
5. (a) $123,541; (b) $18,149

Workout 8
1. 10, 12
2. 15, 18
3. 245, 240
4. 104, 100
5. (a) $9,600; (b) $116,593

Workout 9
1. 519
2. 504
3. 768
4. 1,245
5. About 115 mi

Workout 10
1. 135
2. 304
3. 42
4. 86
5. 10 mi

Workout 11
1. $148
2. $202
3. $0.68
4. $2.84
5. 42

Workout 12
1. $17
2. $104
3. $178
4. $567
5. $1

Workout 13
1. 60,185
2. 48,714
3. 32,000
4. 648,000
5. (a) $113,496; (b) $113,000

Workout 14
1. 9,400
2. 3,200
3. 16,000
4. 19,700
5. 3,200; 9,400; 16,000; 19,700
6. (a) Ferris Wheel: $53,000; The Coaster: $27,200; The Fun House: $19,600; Long Run: $13,600 (b) $13,600; $19,600; $27,200; $53,000

Workout 15
1. 58
2. 12
3. 23
4. 97
5. 9 acres of strawberries, 7 acres of peaches

Workout 16
1. 62
2. 57
3. 116
4. 90
5. wrestling: 4 years, sideshows: 8 years, circuses: 10 years

Workout 17
1. $2,972
2. $4,892
3. $48,670
4. $51,671
5. $74,596

Workout 18
1. $6,023
2. $3,626
3. $1,278
4. $4,697
5. $3,379

Workout 19
1. 1,191
2. 282
3. 1,345
4. 553
5. 915
6. (a) Yes (b) 62 sq ft left

Workout 20
1. 101
2. 135
3. 56
4. 54
5. 16 oz left

Part II: Multiplication

Workout 21
1. 72
2. 204
3. 98
4. 230
5. 185

Workout 22
1. 576
2. 672
3. 150
4. 656
5. 216

Workout 23
1. 1,055
2. 2,142
3. 1,578
4. 5,508
5. 2,064 ft

Workout 24
1. 534
2. 1,068
3. 1,602
4. 2,136
5. 5,340
6. 10,474 peaches

Workout 25
1. 252
2. 268
3. 109
4. 410
5. (a) 1,148 pt (b) 56 pt

Workout 26
1. 832
2. 4,525
3. 309
4. 3,036
5. $2,268

Workout 27
1. 4,500
2. 3,600
3. 600
4. 4,500
5. 2,702 lb

Workout 28
1. 12,192
2. 27,587
3. 2,714
4. 16,947
5. 44,081 lb

Workout 29
1. $1,764
2. $17,640
3. $9,840
4. $7,800
5. $450

Workout 30
1. 330
2. 1,305
3. 5,112
4. 997
5. 1,908

Workout 31
1. 4,199
2. 6,952
3. 46,832
4. 98,796
5. (a) Barn A: 96, Barn B: 72, Barn C: 108; (b) 276 pigs; (c) Barn B, Barn A, Barn C

Workout 32
1. 8,733
2. 2,406
3. 360
4. 81
5. (a) 11,748; (b) 9,348; (c) 2,400

Workout 33
1. 3,088
2. 1,846
3. 7,275
4. 9,072
5. 2,875 days

Workout 34
1. 60
2. 24
3. 56
4. 15
5. 155
6. 48 people

Workout 35
1. 180
2. 231
3. 418
4. 260
5. 312 people

Workout 36
1. 120
2. 102
3. 2,421
4. 51,675
5. 22 nonhorse mounts

Workout 37
1. 6,101
2. 6,642
3. 1,152
4. 918
5. 96 days

Workout 38
1. 6 hours
2. 7 hours
3. 160,000
4. 150,000
5. 120 rides each

Workout 39
1. 17,400
2. 26,000
3. 21,300
4. 36,000
5. 100,700
6. 480 links

Workout 40
1. 252
2. 1,207
3. 1,260
4. 3,906
5. $336

Workout 41
1. 77
2. 60
3. 190
4. 252
5. 21
6. (a) Yes; (b) 60 extra feet

Workout 42
1. $3,000
2. $6,780
3. $2,375
4. $12,848
5. 4697
6. All can be replaced.

Workout 43
1. 348
2. 1,330
3. 312
4. 188
5. 22 times

Workout 44
1. 2,081
2. 1,764
3. 1,472
4. 1,263
5. 2,128 lb

Workout 45
1. $19,743
2. $39,403
3. $67,884
4. $64,074
5. $12,500

Workout 46
1. 1,426
2. 703
3. 2,088
4. 4,524
5. 6,566 ft

Workout 47
1. 42
2. 32
3. 24
4. 23
5. 34 cars

Workout 48
1. $54,537
2. $58,048
3. $171,402
4. $93,906
5. $113,354
6. (a) $147,200; (b) $42,000; (c) $105,200

Part III: Division

Workout 49
1. 6
2. 769
3. 6
4. 9
5. 8 min

Workout 50
1. 134
2. 56
3. 227
4. 121
5. 107 people

Workout 51
1. 20
2. 110
3. 100
4. 200
5. 20 times bigger

Workout 52
1. 21
2. 17
3. 41
4. 12
5. 16 fundraisers

Workout 53
1. 21
2. 50
3. 41
4. 41
5. 51 balloon dogs

Workout 54
1. 21
2. 31
3. 42
4. 82
5. 56 papers

Workout 55
1. 630
2. 390
3. 240
4. 526
5. 190 posters each

Workout 56
1. 320
2. 72
3. 65
4. 54
5. (a) 1,440 total (b) 45 each

Workout 57
1. 596
2. 1,122
3. 52
4. 52
5. 82 riders

Workout 58
1. 53
2. 88
3. 126
4. 123
5. 1,428 strides

Workout 59
1. 20
2. 259
3. 114
4. 314
5. $123

Workout 60
1. 10
2. 20
3. 20
4. 30
5. 4 mph

Part IV: More Multiplication and Division

Workout 61
1. 36
2. 85
3. 16
4. 49
5. 24 people

Workout 62
1. 208
2. 2,704
3. 2,370
4. 13
5. 15 feet per second

Workout 63
1. 4
2. 9
3. 3
4. 4
5. 6 lbs

Workout 64
1. 1,600
2. 1,900
3. 2,300
4. 40
5. 200 yards per second

Workout 65
1. 304
2. 408
3. 306
4. 816
5. 23 gal

Workout 66
1. 156
2. 70
3. 15
4. 47
5. (a) 72 qt; (b) 18 gal

Workout 67
1. 78
2. 48
3. 37
4. 49
5. 864 sq ft

Workout 68
1. 12
2. 30
3. 21
4. 320
5. 240 pies

Workout 69
1. 8
2. 52
3. 4
4. 13
5. 40 yd

Workout 70
1. 4
2. 2
3. 10
4. 14
5. 9 hr

Workout 71
1. 58
2. 44
3. 15
4. 22
5. 21 bags

Workout 72
1. 214
2. 673
3. 57
4. 196
5. 12 hr

Workout 73
1. 42
2. 21
3. 1,253
4. 950
5. 8 ft

Workout 74
1. 210
2. 10,000
3. 24
4. 18
5. 17 ft

Workout 75
1. 19
2. 26
3. 16
4. 15
5. 50 people

Workout 76
1. 0
2. 11
3. 1
4. 1
5. 6 blue pennants

Workout 77
1. 40
2. 24
3. 136
4. 99
5. $20 per ft

Workout 78
1. 67
2. 47
3. 15
4. 5
5. 9 holes

Workout 79
1. 44
2. 130
3. 1,000,000
4. 2,401
5. 22 poles

Workout 80
1. 42
2. 15,625
3. 100
4. 1,225
5. 15 light bulbs

Part V: Fractions

Workout 81
1. ⅓
2. ½
3. ⅘
4. ¾
5. ¼

Workout 82
1. >
2. >
3. <
4. >
5. ⅕

Workout 83
1. $\frac{2}{3}$
2. $\frac{3}{4}$
3. $\frac{7}{10}$
4. 1
5. (a) $\frac{5}{8}$; (b) $\frac{3}{8}$

Workout 84
1. 7
2. 6
3. 8
4. 7
5. 50 ducks

Workout 85
1. $\frac{6}{7}$
2. $\frac{3}{5}$
3. $\frac{3}{5}$
4. $\frac{2}{3}$
5. 19 rooms

Workout 86
1. 1
2. $\frac{1}{2}$
3. $\frac{2}{3}$
4. 1
5. $\frac{1}{6}$

Workout 87
1. $\frac{2}{3}$
2. $\frac{1}{5}$
3. $\frac{4}{5}$
4. $3\frac{5}{8}$
5. $\frac{1}{12}$

Workout 88
1. $4\frac{2}{3}$
2. $2\frac{2}{3}$
3. $7\frac{1}{2}$
4. $6\frac{3}{4}$
5. $1\frac{1}{2}$ in.

Workout 89
1. $3\frac{1}{3}$
2. $3\frac{1}{4}$
3. $2\frac{1}{2}$
4. $2\frac{1}{7}$
5. $2\frac{1}{2}$ lb

Workout 90
1. 2
2. 2
3. 1
4. $6\frac{1}{2}$
5. 80 min

Workout 91
1. $\frac{1}{2}$
2. $\frac{9}{10}$
3. $\frac{5}{8}$
4. $\frac{1}{9}$
5. $\frac{1}{14}$

Workout 92
1. $\frac{1}{4}$
2. $\frac{1}{5}$
3. $1\frac{1}{4}$
4. $5\frac{1}{6}$
5. 6 bags

Workout 93
1. $2\frac{1}{10}$
2. $\frac{1}{8}$
3. $6\frac{5}{24}$
4. $\frac{3}{16}$
5. $15\frac{1}{4}$ rolls

Workout 94
1. $26\frac{3}{16}$
2. $2\frac{1}{6}$
3. $3\frac{1}{9}$
4. $2\frac{23}{24}$
5. $9\frac{7}{8}$ in.

Workout 95
1. $8\frac{11}{24}$
2. $4\frac{1}{24}$
3. $\frac{1}{12}$
4. $13\frac{1}{12}$
5. $3\frac{1}{12}$ boxes

Workout 96
1. 3
2. 4
3. $2\frac{7}{8}$
4. $\frac{17}{24}$
5. $13\frac{1}{2}$ in.

Workout 97
1. $\frac{7}{12}$
2. $1\frac{3}{5}$
3. $3\frac{5}{6}$
4. $4\frac{5}{16}$
5. $1\frac{7}{16}$ tanks

Workout 98
1. 2 hrs.
2. $2\frac{1}{2}$ hr
3. $3\frac{1}{3}$ hr
4. $8\frac{3}{4}$ hr
5. $5\frac{3}{4}$ hr

Workout 99
1. 90 min
2. 198 min
3. 130 min
4. 340 min
5. 30 times

Workout 100
1. $5\frac{1}{8}$ ft
2. $6\frac{23}{24}$
3. $12\frac{11}{12}$
4. $17\frac{1}{16}$
5. $13\frac{1}{4}$ ft

Part VI: Decimals

Workout 101
1. 15.5
2. 34.1
3. $26.54
4. $59.66
5. $146.79

Workout 102
1. 66.5
2. 304.8
3. $111.48
4. 87.59
5. $59.34

Workout 103
1. 19,789.21
2. 27.79
3. $31.52
4. 30.85
5. $25,024.70

Workout 104
1. 1.121
2. 69.0012
3. 43.235
4. 790.32
5. 4.482 m

Workout 105
1. >
2. <
3. 14.1
4. 17.03
5. Yes

Workout 106
1. 1.86
2. 4.5
3. 12.19
4. 3.005
5. 1.435 m

Workout 107
1. $1,252.83
2. 111.929
3. 34.88
4. 4.776
5. $595.51

Workout 108
1. 2.30
2. 88.97
3. 92.4502
4. 798.12
5. 9.17 cm

Workout 109
1. 13.574
2. 11.0929
3. 2.4
4. 105.625
5. $25.82

Workout 110
1. 29.22
2. $32.82
3. 283.773
4. 455.197
5. $161.25

Workout 111
1. 1,717.4
2. 1,749.84
3. 1.254
4. 1.947
5. (a) 1,230 people; (b) $2,214

Workout 112
1. 50
2. 14
3. $11.07
4. $10.96
5. $5.25

Workout 113
1. $2.50
2. $6.29
3. $8.13
4. $19.33
5. $3.75 per child

Workout 114
1. 1.5
2. 2.34
3. $4.70
4. $38.89
5. $15.60

Workout 115
1. $7
2. 2,000
3. 6,000
4. $14,000
5. $13,500

Workout 116
1. $9.72
2. $67.44
3. $19.84
4. 47.634
5. %501.60

Workout 117
1. 144
2. 90
3. 239.82
4. 480
5. 162 pies

Workout 118
1. 36.5
2. 0.36
3. $8.40
4. $16.64
5. $9.60

Workout 119
1. 0.2
2. 8
3. 40.2
4. 1.02
5. 9 min

Workout 120
1. 0.2
2. 2
3. 40.3
4. 28
5. 15 times longer

Part VII: Mixed Practice for Math Review

Workout 121
1. 4,000
2. 42,000
3. 110,000
4. 500,000
5. $800,000

Workout 122
1. 45
2. 49
3. 75
4. 108
5. 92 days

Workout 123
1. $1,680
2. $2,430
3. $1,704
4. $4,200
5. $5,115

Workout 124
1. $20.40
2. $52
3. $90.30
4. $100.90
5. $90.50

Workout 125

1. 78.5
2. 62.8
3. 83.25
4. 105.6
5. 124 ft

Workout 126

1. $143
2. $233
3. $370
4. $602
5. $762

Workout 127

1. 2,420
2. 3,960
3. 1,923
4. 2,238
5. 24 races

Workout 128

1. 10, 16, 24, 34
2. 52, 64, 71, 98
3. 130, 123, 110, 94
4. 98, 96, 85, 75
5. Insert Table 10 Here

Workout 129

1. 36
2. 14
3. 24
4. 56
5. 6 min

Workout 130

1. 8,000
2. 12,000
3. 15,000
4. 3,125
5. $20,000

About the Author

To say that mathematics changed Michael Cain's life would be an understatement. The long road he took to get to the point where he is now started as an art student. He got his first degree from a rather bohemian art school in Pittsburgh, PA. The school has long since disappeared but the experiences and instruction he received there still plays a major role in his life. With encouragement from his mother, he pursued a second degree. It was at a local community college where he discovered his mathematics aptitude. Mathematics put an order to and changed his art for the better. Seeing what mathematics had done for his life, he decided to become a teacher and help others find the joy and the transformative power of mathematics

Cain has been teaching for more than 20 years and writing mathematical supplements for just as long. He started by creating small booklets for use by his students. Cain could see that imaginative storytelling and interesting characters engaged his students. He sent his work to publishers and was able to land his first job with *Scholastic Math* Magazine. Since then, he has preformed on camera as the instructed for the "One to One Basic Math" series, written a number of mathematical supplements, and created thousands of online educational materials. He is the creator of highly acclaimed "Absurd Math" online math game.

Between a teaching career, a thriving education business, and a numerous exhibitions of his works of art, Cain still finds time to have a family. The father of three teenage boys and a 4-year-old daughter, Cain enjoys the support of his wife and the love of his family as he continues to pursue his dreams of education, writing, and art. To see some of Cain's online creations, go to http://www.tower23.com.